Earl and Norma Morgan

# Against All Odds I'm Still Here

*From A Meaningless Existence On The Streets To A*
*Purpose Filled Life With God*

Earl and Norma Morgan

# Against All Odds I'm Still Here

Earl is available to share his story. To book him:

Email: againstalloddsimstillhere@gmail.com

Website: againstalloddsimstillhere.com

Front and back photos by James@bellphoto.co.uk

All Bible references are from the New International Version (NIV)

First published in 2019 by Earl and Norma Morgan
Copyright © June, 2018 Earl and Norma Morgan. All rights reserved.

**ISBN: 978-1-909389-23-6**

Earl and Norma Morgan

# Against All Odds I'm Still Here

*From A Meaningless Existence On The Streets To A Purpose Filled Life With God*

# Against All Odds I'm Still Here

First published by Earl and Norma Morgan

January, 2019

# Dedication

This book is dedicated to my grandparents Festus and Mardie Mckenzie for their godly input in my life.

To Norma, my beautiful wife

# Contents

# Acknowledgements

Firstly, I want to thank my Lord and Saviour Jesus Christ, without you I would not be here. Thank you Jesus for being with me, for protecting me, for blessing my life and for enabling me to complete this book.

To my wife Norma, thank you for standing with me throughout my journey. Thank you for being there for me, for encouraging me to write my story, working tirelessly on this project, sacrificing so much to enable me to achieve this goal. Other than Jesus Christ, you are the reason I live. I love you Babes and always will x

To my family, the Morgans, the McKenzies, the Akinyemi's, the Morrises and the Fergusons. Thank you for your love, prayers and support. I love you all.

To all my friends and church family, there are too many to mention by name, but you know who you are and what you have done. Thank you for praying for and supporting us on our journey. I love you all.

To every organ donor and the families who have lost loved ones but have consented to donate their organs. Thank you! Thank you! Thank you!

To all the NHS staff at Oxford, Northampton and Milton Keynes, particularly the Renal staff for the dedicated work that you do each day. Thank you!

To Kwame MA McPherson, for your input in helping to organise this book. Thank you Sir.

# Foreword

I first met Earl Morgan twenty years ago when he and his wife, Norma, relocated from London to Milton Keynes where I was living and we soon became very good friends. After getting to know him, what struck me most was his love for God, his love for his wife and his strong desire to share his faith with whoever he met. Over the years, Earl has had many health issues but they have never stopped him; even when hospitalized, he continued to share the good news of Jesus Christ with those around him.

His faith in his God and his positive attitude even when facing death has been an inspiration to many and something admired by all who know him. The seventeen years since being diagnosed with cancer, in 2000, until his kidney transplant in 2017 and so much more has been beautifully documented in this interesting and factual book.

And after reading this amazing story, you will agree with me when I say that miracles are not just things of the past but they do still happen, even today. Earl's story will encourage and inspire you to believe that with God's help you too can face life's challenges and overcome them. I am so grateful to God that against all odds my friend Earl Morgan is still here.

*Ruby Blake*
A Dear Friend

# Introduction

When I decided to write this book - my life story – I had no idea what I would say, what it would look like or how it would read. I was new to writing, much less to writing a book, but here I am. I have done it with the help of my beautiful wife, Norma. As you will read throughout my life God has led me, guiding me along even when I had no idea that He was doing so. Unscathed, through all my various experiences only confirmed, even more so, how much He played a massive part in my life and the miracle of having a kidney to continue my life, shows how much more I need to praise Him, and let others know of His unlimited power.

*Against All Odds, I'm Still Here* takes you into my life, letting you understand and appreciate the love I have received from all around me, especially from God and it is my hope that it inspires you to believe more so than what you do now, that you too can overcome whatever you are facing or going through.

*Earl*

# Chapter 1 - Early Life

My name is Earl Livingstone Morgan; I was born on 23rd July 1953 to Vivien and Edna Morgan in Mitchell Town, Clarendon, Jamaica in the small community of Vere.

It was a lovely rural community; everyone knew each other and would share whatever they had. Harvest time was particularly nice as it was the season for giving and receiving that which the land had produced.

I am one of seven children and have two sisters and four brothers.

When I was two and a half years old, my parents decided to leave me in Jamaica with my grandparents Festus and Mardie McKenzie and relocate to England in the hope of finding a better life for us and for themselves. Their intention was that my older brother Carlton and I would join them at a later stage. So in January 1956, my parents boarded a ship bound for England.

This separation was quite traumatic initially, but as time went by, I adjusted well to the situation and being so young, as far as I was concerned, my grandparents were my parents.

Being the first and only grandchild in the McKenzie household was fun; my brother lived with my father's parents, Vincent and Marion Morgan, approximately twenty miles away, so I received all the attention and treats from my grandparents and was never in need of anything. I was well looked after. Many would say that I was spoilt but I would rather say that I was blessed since both sets of grandparents would often fuss over who should have me at any given time but the McKenzie's always seemed to win, so most of my time was spent with them which meant I became very attached.

My grandparents' successful food supply business meant that they were not badly off financially and were well respected in the community. They were Christians and always helped others in whichever way they could. Looking back, I can see just how much influence they had on my life by showing me real Christian values. They ensured that I attended Sunday school - which I loved. In fact, I enjoyed it so much that from the age of four *(so I was told)* I began telling my friends about Jesus and brought them to church with me.

Although I was so young, it was obvious that the hand of God was in my life.

Although my parents lived in the UK and I in Jamaica, they never forgot about me. Mum would often send gifts for me, especially at Christmas. I can remember my excitement at receiving my very own tin of Quality Street chocolates which I would share with my school friends, taking great delight in boasting about where they came from.

Eventually, I started attending Mitchell Town Primary School and settled in very well with the other children. Being a very friendly child, I never lacked friends and my two best friends were Solomon Reid and Ernest Watson. And since my family were well known, no one ever tried fighting or taking advantage of me as they knew they would have to answer to my grandmother, in particular. I was the "apple of her eyes". I always felt safe and remembered that at the end of every school day, whenever I went out to the gates, my grandma would be there waiting for me.

As I grew older, my grandmother taught me how to cook, clean and wash; skills I would certainly need later in life. *It is amazing just how God seems to prepare us for what is ahead without us even realising it.*

After primary school, I started at secondary. I felt really grown up because by this time I had my very own bicycle and there was no need for grandma to wait for me after school anymore. Now, I could make my own way home. It was scary since this was a new responsibility for me but I loved it. I loved putting on my uniform, waving goodbye to my family knowing I had my own money in my pocket and could stop at the local shop before arriving at school, buying 'Staggerback' sweets; a very unusual name for sweets but they were my favourite. I was so pleased that I was able to buy sweets and share them with my classmates. Life in Jamaica was fun.

Because I was a very popular pupil, my teachers soon recognised my sporting abilities. I loved playing cricket *(I still enjoy watching it even now)* and was a very good all-rounder. It was a privilege to be appointed as the school cricket team captain. I remember playing a memorable game when I scored my first century on home soil against another school team. My performance helped my team to win the competition and we received a really nice trophy.

I was also made the district captain.

To say I was excited, is an understatement. Not only was I selected as the school and district team captain, I was sent on special training courses to help develop my skills and was being considered to play for my country's junior team by the Jamaican West Indies Selecting Board. It was at this age – fifteen - that I received a letter from my parents stating that the time had come for me to join them in the UK. Although I was greatly disappointed at losing the opportunity to excel and pursue my sporting dreams of becoming a world class cricketer, I was happy at the thought of reuniting with my parents.

After receiving the letter, it took approximately one year to obtain all the relevant documentation I would need. Finally, on one Saturday evening in May 1969, I boarded a Pan-Am aeroplane at Norman Manley International Airport, Kingston. There were thirty-four children on board including myself who were travelling to the UK to meet up with our parents; like me, some even had chaperones, organised by our parents to ensure our safe arrival. This was my first time flying and so, I had nothing to compare it with and as far as I was concerned, everything seemed fine and eventually, the following day, we arrived in the UK.

At Heathrow Airport, I disembarked and my chaperone who had been with me, sorted everything for me. She spoke to the Immigration Officer on my behalf and collected my luggage. She never left me until I was handed over to my mother and as much as my mother and Carlton, *(my brother, who had left Jamaica two years prior, also came to meet me)*, were happy to see me, I was really grateful at seeing them again. Now, my only thoughts were how I longed to be back in the beautiful Jamaican sunshine because here, in London, United Kingdom, it was so cold.

## Chapter 2 - Dark Days

The flight from Jamaica to the UK was exciting. Growing up I often heard adults talk about what it was like being on an aeroplane, so for me, this being my first time flying meant I would finally experience what they had spoken about. However, I had not realised just how long the flight would be; it was in fact nine and a half hours but it being so long, allowed me the time to think about what was about to happen to me. You see, I was two and a half years of age when my parents left me and now I was sixteen and so my emotions were all over the place. Though thrilled, I was also apprehensive and scared at the thought of meeting up with two people who were now strangers to me. My mind raced. How would our first meeting be after all these years apart? Would I affectionately embrace them or would I just extend my hand for a formal handshake? Would there be tears of joy or some other emotion? It was hard to say and nonetheless, even though there was no hugging with my mother who came to meet me, our reunion went as well as could be expected. She said, politely: *"Hello son."* Thankfully, my brother and I embraced, making our reunion easier to deal with.

As we progressed home, I remember looking out of the car window at the many buildings with smoke coming out of the chimneys and commenting to my mother about how many factories there were; she smiled and corrected me by saying: *"Son, those are not factories; they're houses where people live."* I was amazed because in Jamaica only factories had chimneys.

When I had landed, I expected both of my parents to meet me but to my dismay, my father was not there. I was extremely disappointed since I had really hoped to see him. Soon after my arrival, I was made to learn from my mother that she and my father were no longer together but they had separated a few years earlier and were going through the final stages of a divorce. I was devastated and disappointed that I had not been told about this before, but my mother said that neither she nor my father wanted to tell me via a letter, so that was the reason why she waited until I had arrived in the UK before letting me know. I was angry because I loved them both equally but I knew I would have to accept what had happened and go and live with my mother. As nothing was explained to me, I was not interested in finding out anything concerning my mother's new relationship. Not having my father around was really hard for me to deal with; I was upset to say the least. I felt my parent's divorce was cruel on me. I felt I was a victim, torn in two, confused by the awful pain that the situation brought to our family. I sometimes found myself withdrawing from people around me as I tried to deal with my inward pain but I was never out of control of me. I made sure of that.

Anyway, God helped me and I say it was God because I know I could not have coped with the separation by myself. Eventually, I accepted the situation and as time passed, I adjusted accordingly by continuing to attend church as I had done back in Jamaica and started planning for my future.

In 1970, I began attending Brixton College and was doing well with my studies. By this time, my mother had re-married but in spite of this, we had developed a very close relationship by spending quality time together, just talking and making up for those lost years I guess. Going shopping at Brixton market was always one of our favourite times together as mother and son; we were always together. I was so happy. Then, unexpectedly, something happened.

My mother became very ill and could no longer work, so I gave up college and began working in order to support us. By now, the man she had married was no longer in our lives as things did not work out between them. I was never happy about mum's new relationship, and therefore never really regarded her new husband as my step-father but I still made the effort to be polite and respectful towards him. Our relationship was one of mutual respect and understanding but that was as far as it went.

Between 1971 and 1982, I began working various jobs, from being an Office Clerk to working on a building site; in general, I always got on well with my work colleagues and just did what I had to do in order to earn a living which would enable me, manage the household bills while at the same time, care for my mother. As you can imagine, this was not easy and when I was in the prime of life, my world was turned upside down. In 1982, after years of sickness, my beloved mother died.

# Chapter 3 - Street Life

It was as this point in my life that I began to lose my faith in God since many questions raced through and occupied my mind. How could God allow this to happen? If He was so good, kind and loving, why had he let my mother suffer and eventually die at the early age of fifty-two.

My mother, who I adored, was now gone. My mother the one always praying and believing in God. The one who would pray for me whenever I went out. So why? Why? Why? What made it worse was that I could no longer afford the upkeep of the house in  which we lived and whatever financial help we were receiving from the government while my mother was alive had now stopped. I now found myself almost homeless but thank God for my long time dear friend, Joe, who allowed me to live at one of his properties rent free until I was able to get back on my feet. Yet, in spite of his help, life seemed to have no meaning; I was angry, frustrated and emotionally drained. So, I stopped attending church and in my frustration decided to hit the streets as that seemed to be the only way that I could deal with my pain and survive. Clubbing, partying, girls, alcohol and drugs became the norm for me. I guess I was searching for answers but in the wrong places.

I will pause for a moment and speak to someone whose world may have been turned upside down by some unexpected tragedy as mine was. Someone once said: *"Life is not fair; good things sometimes happen to bad people and bad things sometimes happen to good people."* This is so true and yes we do sometime question God concerning the terrible things that come our way. Whether you believe in God or not, the truth remains that Jesus Christ loves you. The way God may allow things to pan out is often beyond our human ability to understand but don't lose hope, don't give up. He will help you if you call out to Him.

While I was doing the things I was doing, I often found myself thinking about God and what would happen if I died in that state and that thought terrified me.

Many times I would be at a party, the music blaring and people dancing and I would find myself standing in a corner, observing them as they enjoyed themselves; yet, I was not. Often, I would leave a party in the early hours of a Sunday morning and find myself in a church. God was dealing with me and He was not about to let me go; my life was a torment as I tried so hard to forget about Him. I was angry with Him and blamed Him for what had happened to my mother. I was also angry with life I no longer cared about what happened to me. So, eventually, I became a drug-baron and started to make a lot of money, so much so that I employed a chauffeur and had four people working for me. By doing this, it gave me a sense of power and control of my own life since I had no control over what had happened to my mother. It was at this point that I began using the name "Chuckie". Incidentally, I was given this name by a Jamaican reggae artist called I'Roy who had come over to the UK to do a tour in the eighties. "Chuckie" was the title of a reggae song and also a dance groove that followed the release of that song. Since I was a good dancer, the name just fit. I also joined a gang and we called ourselves the "Untouchables" as we felt that we were indeed untouchable by both the police and other gangs.

Soon after our gang established itself, gaining the reputation of being ruthless; in fact, we were more than just a street gang, we were mafias and this was a well-known fact among other gangs. Life on the streets was extremely dangerous because of rival gangs. We had to know how to protect ourselves and so we did whatever was necessary in order to survive and carrying a gun was a necessity. There were many occasions when I pulled my gun but God had

always been good to me, in that even though I was not serving Him, He never allowed me to use it to hurt anyone.

I clearly remember one particular incident.

I was at a party in Birmingham and a dispute broke out between myself and another man over a drug deal gone wrong. I was so angry with him that I pulled out my loaded gun and pointed it at his chest. I then pulled the trigger three times but nothing happened. When the man realised my gun had jammed, he turned and ran, leaving one shoe behind. I chased after him but he got away. I then went to the rear of the building and pointed my gun to the sky. I pulled the trigger and to my amazement, it fired. That night I saw that God was definitely on my case because had He not intervened, I would have probably killed that man and my God-given purpose in life would have been aborted.

Street life may have seemed glamorous, initially, but having to live a life where I was constantly looking over my shoulders, not knowing who was coming up behind me or for what reason, was no fun. The threat of being robbed at any given time whether by an angry, desperate drug user or by a jealous rival gang member became so real. Also, being stopped and searched by the police was a regular thing in London in those days. Plus, there was no one that I could really trust and thus fear was my real friend and death, a close companion, but all I really wanted to be was happy again. Just to be at peace with myself and with the world, but those feeling seemed to evade me no matter how hard I tried. I could not turn to my family because other than my brother Carlton, no one else knew the depth to which I had fallen.

For many years, I continued on this path, during which time I became a reggae music promoter. Being a very sociable person, this lifestyle suited me just fine as it meant that I met many reggae artists such as Papa San - now a Christian himself - Peter Tosh, Bob Marley, Dennis Brown and so on. With my brother Carlton, who like myself had turned away from God and was using the street name, "Jah Paul", *(he returned to serving the Lord some years later and continued in the role of Pastor and Bishop of Grace International Miracle Ministries in London until his death in 2016),* we became involved with several sound systems such as "Count Shelley", "Coxsone" and "Frontline International".

Those who may have been involved with reggae music in the 70's and 80's may remember those names. I was the MC who worked side by side with the DJ's at various functions. We hosted many club dances, house parties and live shows bringing artists over from Jamaica and America to perform; these events were always well attended and my life was so busy. I was out just about every weekend, travelling the length and breadth of the country but yet still, there was emptiness inside me.

On Friday 10th April 1981, our Sound System – a travelling disco - known as Frontline International, was due to play at Brixton Town Hall. As most of the guys involved were familiar with the area, we decided to meet in the afternoon at the West Indian Club on Railton Road, which was not too far from the Town Hall, so that we could just chill out and relax a bit before the show started later that evening. We were so excited because we knew that the promotion we had done, would draw a capacity crowd of five to six hundred people.

Brixton in those days was an area with serious social and economic problems and as such it was not a strange thing for a black youth to be stopped and searched by the police without even having committed a crime. There were several of these incidences which had occurred in the area, causing tension between the police and the black community. This made it necessary for the heavy police presence on the streets; but, although, this may have been necessary, it was met with great objection by the community.

At around 6:00pm, while still at the club, we became aware of a commotion going on outside; it turned out that a crowd of black youths had gathered around two police officers who the crowd felt had mishandled an injured black youth. As tension was already high, it did not take long for things to escalate out of control; and although extra police were drafted in, soon, over 300 angry youths had converged on the area and were rioting mercilessly. For me, I found myself getting involved by torching cars, throwing bricks and petrol bombs and eventually having to run for my life from the riot police.

This violence went on for three days and it became so bad that the whole area was on lock-down, no-one could get out and no-one could get in, this included the emergency services. It was reported that between that Friday and Sunday, 299 police were injured along with 65 members of the public and there were 82 arrests  made. I was eventually able to escape only because I had a friend who lived in the area, and whose house I was able to hide in until the Monday morning, by which time the police had gained full control of the situation.

Looking back, I can see how God protected me even when I was doing that which was so wrong.

# Chapter 4 – The Torment

God constantly plagued my mind with thoughts that I should return to serving Him as that was how I was brought up and that I should not be doing the things I was doing at that time. I was now in my early 30's but my life seemed to be on a downward spiral. There was such a war going on inside me and though I wanted God, I was not ready to forsake or give up my lifestyle. It was a life I had become accustom to but the battle was real. So, I intensified everything that I was doing in an attempt to prove to myself and those around me that I was in control of my own life and that I could live the way I wanted to without being accountable to a higher being, I would party even harder than before; be excessive with my spending by buying expensive clothes, shoes and cars not because I really needed them but because I knew that I could afford them. All of this was to mask what I was really feeling inside.

God has a purpose for each and every one of us as it is stated in the Bible, in Romans chapter 11, verse 29: *"For God's gifts and His call are irrevocable."* (NIV) So, even if an individual turned away from God in rebellion or through sheer disobedience as I had done, the mandate on that person's life and the torment to follow would continue until they surrendered to God's will. For me, that mandate was to tell people about the love God had for them. He made things so uncomfortable for me that even while clubbing and trying to have a so-called "good time" I found myself telling others that they needed to be in church - what a contradiction that was! Here I was away from God but yet still encouraging others to turn to God. I would often party from Friday night right through to Sunday morning, leave the club then make my way to church. Many times, whenever I found myself sitting in the back row of a particular church in Stoke Newington in London, I felt condemned because I knew I was living a double life and that I needed to make a decision. I would try to slip into the back of the church and others would look at me in an accusatory way; perhaps it was the smell of the alcohol and drugs on me which repulsed them but that was not what I needed. Within me, I already felt condemned and what I really needed was love. I needed help to make the transition. Having said that, I remember one particular old lady who would come and pat me on my shoulder and say: *"It's alright son, you just keep on coming."* She seemed to look right through me, knowing exactly where I was in my life and although she had not condoned my wrong-doings, in her approach, I always felt the love of God whenever she spoke with me.

It's easy to be judgmental of others who have not measured up to our so-called "standard of righteousness", but it was for this very reason that Jesus said to the religious folks of His day in St. John, chapter 8, verse 7[b]: ***"Let any one of you who is without sin be the first to throw a stone at her"*** (NIV), when they brought a woman to Him and said she was caught in the very act of adultery and expecting Him to condemn her to death as the Mosaic Law demanded *(please read Leviticus, chapter 20, verse 10)* but in His mercy, Jesus forgave her by saying: ***"Go now and leave your life of sin."*** (NIV)

Looking back, I can see how much of what I went through, was a result of my own stubbornness and that I was inflicting mental and emotion pain on myself.

# Chapter 5 – Near Misses

There were many occasions when I could have ended up in jail or even worst been killed while being involved with "street life".

*Teddy Boys*

During the 70's and 80's, Skinheads and the National Front movement were in full swing; these groups of white youths detested black youths, who they called "Jamaican Rude Boys".

In 1987, after spending a Friday evening playing snooker at a club in Stratford, I was walking home alone in the early hours of Saturday morning when I became aware of six white youths coming towards me. Instantly I knew what was about to happen; one black youth up against six white youths. I was in serious trouble.

As they approached, they suddenly attacked and as I looked into their eyes I could see their hatred and racial prejudice they felt towards me. I was terrified. In those days, I practiced Kung Fu so I tried defending myself, thinking that if I could at least take one of them out then perhaps the others would run off, giving me a chance to escape. As the first youth came at me, I attempted to kick him in the head knowing that if I did get him, he would have been out cold; I put every effort into the kick but, unfortunately I missed and fell flat on my back hitting my head on the concrete. Although dazed and on the ground I was aware that one of them was heading my way with a broken bottle in his hand while the others were kicking and punching me. He had the intention of stabbing me in my chest, probably through my heart but somehow I managed to grab his hand which stopped the full impact of the broken bottle. I was stabbed, how badly I was not sure but at this point they ran off, leaving me for dead.

As blood poured from the wound in my chest, I knew that if I didn't get help I would die and I certainly did not want to die like that; on some street, my blood staining the pavement. The pain was excruciating, nearly causing unconsciousness. I was losing so much blood and becoming weaker and weaker by the second; my whole life flashed before me - what I'd done and what I'd yet to do. My vision was blurring. Strangely enough though, the thought of not knowing if my attackers had really gone or if they were still in the area just waiting to finish me off, seemed to give me the strength I needed to get up and stagger towards some houses I could just about see in the distance. I have no idea how far I managed to walk or crawl but I know that I never made it to the houses. I collapsed in the nearby park.

I eventually woke up in a hospital room.

An amazing part of this story was relayed to me some days later by the doctors and nurses who cared for me at Whitechapel Hospital in London and also by family members who kept a bedside vigil until I regained consciousness; two days after my ordeal.

There was a lady who lived in the area where I was attacked. She usually walked her dog between 5:00am - 6:00am but on this particular morning her dog became agitated and started barking at around 3:00am so she decided to get up early and take her out. It was while she was walking that she saw me lying on the ground in a pool of blood and raised the alarm. The doctors also told me that if I'd stayed there for just a few minutes longer, I would most certainly have bled to death as the bottle stab was very close to my heart.

I don't remember the precious lady's name but I do remember her visiting me while in hospital and would just like to thank her for saving my life and more importantly I thank God for using the dog to alert her owner that something was wrong.

*Drug Deal Gone Bad*

On one occasion while I was involved with drugs, I was standing on a particular street in Stoke Newington, London when a car pulled up close to me, with the front passenger side window down and it stopped. The driver lent across and asked me if I had any drugs; to which I hastily replied yes. At this point, the driver opened the car door. I was eager to get this sale as there were so many other dealers close by, so I jumped into the car which immediately sped off. The car moved off at such a speed that the door seem to automatically close itself and to my horror I heard a click which meant that someone had locked the door. I knew I was in big trouble.

I was not aware until a few minutes later that there was someone else hiding in the rear of the car. We travelled for about two minutes and then turned unto a very deserted road. I suddenly felt the barrel of a gun being held to the back of my head. It was so cold as the man pressed it against my skin while he demanded that I handed over everything I had in my possession which was drugs, money and jewellery. Although I gave him everything I had on me, the gun was still pressed against the back of my head so I knew that there was absolutely nothing I could do to stop him from pulling the trigger.

Because I was always a good talker, the only thing I could think of doing was talk my way out of the situation. So, although I was petrified, I tried being as calm as I possibly could be and began talking to him. I said: *"You don't want to do this; what good would it do for you to kill me and then have to spend the rest of your life in jail?"* It was at this point that I no longer felt the gun at my head and immediately the driver stopped the car in the middle of the road, unlocked the door and shouted at me saying *"Get out."* As I got out, they sped off. I was so relieved and grateful that my life was spared yet again.

*The Near Fatal Car Crash*

Back in those days, it was the "in thing" to have a fast car; although I didn't drive I would buy nice cars like the V8 Rover and the Capri and have someone chauffeur me around. My brother Carlton however had a BMW 6 series vehicle. We would often travel at high speed, in excess of one hundred miles per hour on the motorway from London to various parts of the country to attend different shows or to host them ourselves. It was the norm for us to do that and we thought it was fun but looking back now, I can see just how foolish we were.

Whenever we hit the road, there was always a convoy of cars following us, friends who would accompany us wherever we went and although I was not a Christian at that time, I always prayed for protection before travelling. Also I knew my dad, who at that time was a Pastor, constantly prayed for my brother and I and because many of the guys who were with us knew this, they preferred to travel in the car I was in.

On one particular occasion, while travelling on the M1 motorway returning from Birmingham, a car full of white youths overtook us and so we began chasing them; as I was in the front passenger seat, I glanced at the speedometer and noticed we were travelling at one hundred and twenty miles per hour. My brother, our driver, was in deep in concentration when suddenly our front tyre blew out. I remember thinking: *"This is it, we're dead"* as the car swerved and shook. It shuddered as the tyre struggled to re-inflate and Carlton struggled to control the vehicle. Amazingly for us, the road was clear as Carlton regained his handling, veering from the fast lane over into a lay-by without us turning over. I concluded that the experience was a miracle and that the angel of God was guiding our car that night.

*The Day My Friend Died Before My Eyes*

After years of living dangerously and the many close shaves with death, the turning point finally came in 1993. My brother Carlton was hosting a function at a club in Hackney, London. He was expecting a large crowd so extra drinks were needed and he needed a car to transport them to the club. He decided to ask my dad if he could use his car for the night since he lived nearby.

Earlier that evening, a friend and I went for a meal. I was dressed to a "T" in my beaver hat, expensive suit, crombi coat and crocodile skin shoes, plus lots of jewellery. We both usually carried guns for our protection, but because we knew we were going to my brother's function afterwards, we decided that we would not take our guns into the club but would bury them in the garden at the rear of the venue until after the function was over. So after our meal, we made our way to the club and did exactly as we had planned and bury our guns.

By this time Carlton was already at the venue sorting things out so when my friend and I arrived, I left him by the bar and went with my brother in a taxi, to collect dad's car. My dad was a godly man, Pastor and a praying man. As we left the house with the keys to his car, the last thing he said to us was: *"I'm going inside to pray for you two."*

We returned to the club and I headed towards the bar where my friend was waiting. We ordered drinks. The bar was located near the entrance of the hall and I was standing closest to it. After a while we heard a commotion by the door and suddenly three men entered; looked at us and said to my friend: *"It's you we've come for."* At that point they aim guns at us and fired three shots.

As I was closest to them, the bullets literally grazed my coat, hitting my friend in his chest. He collapsed to the floor as I tried to grab him. I didn't see the men make good their escape since I was more concerned about my friend. Blood covered his chest and he was finding it difficult to breathe.

My friend was dying before my eyes but again I saw the hand of God in my life because, though everything happened very quickly, if I had my gun with me at that time I would have pulled it and perhaps killed those guys and could have ended up serving a triple–life sentence for murder.

My brother and I picked up the almost lifeless body of my friend and headed for Hackney Hospital. I remember holding my friend's head in my lap, speaking with him to stay conscious, trying to keep him alive. Throughout the ten-minute journey to the hospital I never heard him utter a word and sadly, after reaching the hospital and after every effort from the doctors to save his life, he died. I don't know if he had the chance to call out to Jesus in those last moments, but witnessing his death caused me to take stock of my own life and cry out to God as I sat on the bench outside the hospital. I remember saying: *"Jesus, thank you for sparing my life, I'm coming home."*

That night, I could not sleep; in fact, sleep was the last thing on my mind. Yes, I was physically and emotionally exhausted, angry and sad, but how could I sleep? One of my closest friends had just been killed in a horrific manner, which I later found out was a case of mistaken identity. All I wanted to do at that point was to be in church, surrounded by peaceful people.

After this incident, the reality dawned on me that I really needed to have God in my life and if I didn't change course, I too could end up dead.

Seeing what happened to my friend was a defining moment for me.

## Chapter 6 – The Transition

As time went by, I regularly attended church. I made the decision that I wanted to change my life and although I had stopped drinking, doing drugs and partying and was now working legitimately, I still struggled with the temptation to return to what I was used to. It was not helped with the phone calls and invites which kept coming from my associates. My transformation did not occur overnight.

Although we are responsible for our actions, who we associate with can influence our decisions, whether they be good or bad ones.

After a few years had passed, I was now forty-two-years-old and by this stage I had three children from my previous relationships. I was not proud of my past but if my story helps anyone, then so be it. I lived in a big house with a lady in London but things were not working out between us because we were on different paths. We no longer wanted the same things and lived separate lives. One evening, while at home relaxing and listening to some Gospel music I suddenly heard a voice speaking to me. It was in my ear and throughout my inner being. It said: ***"Son if you want*** *me, come now."* It rolled like thunder and I knew it was God; I did not hesitate and ran upstairs, opened the wardrobe, grabbed a handful of clothes and sprinted out of the house. I had nowhere to go but a few moments later as I was walking away, the same voice spoke again: *"Don't ever go back."* At that point, the only person I could think of who could help me was my brother Carlton who was now a Pastor. I saw a call box and found some coins in my pocket. I called him and he came for me.

I stayed with my brother and his wife for six months, sleeping on the couch or floor since they only had a one-bedroomed apartment; this however was God's doing because I needed their spiritual help as I was transitioning from street life to Christ. Because everything I had, I left behind, looking to start all over again. My life became challenging. Imagine what that was like. I really had attained a comfortable lifestyle, yet here I was at forty-two with nothing to my name except the clothes I had managed to hold in my arms when I ran, leaving my home. There were many of my friends and some family members who encouraged me to return, get my things and sell the house but how could I when God had ordered me not to go back. *"Don't go back"* were His exact words.

One day, while sitting in my brother's apartment, I found myself reflecting on all the things I had lost; the expensive things which remained behind when I walked away. The more I pondered on this, the angrier I became. Why was I sleeping on my brother's couch or sometimes on the floor when I had my own comfortable bed in my own house? If I could no longer have and enjoy all the things I had hustled for, then why should someone else enjoy them? With these thoughts racing through my mind, I decided to go back.

I headed to a nearby petrol station with a five litre can, filling it with petrol. I wrapped it in a plastic bag, paid and then got on a bus to my old house; my intention was to pour the petrol through the letter box and burn it down. As I sat on the bus thinking about what I was about to do, I suddenly realised I had almost missed my stop. I jumped up and in my haste got off the bus forgetting the can of petrol which I had placed under the seat. The bus drove off but as it would happen, another bus came from the opposite direction, which would take me back to where my brother was living. So I crossed the road, hopped on that bus and went back home. That was God.

Many people gave me three months, some said I would not last six-month as a Christian, but twenty-three years later, all praise to God, I am still a Christian.

# Chapter 7 - A New Start

As God had spoken so profoundly to me, I walked out of my house, leaving behind, everything that represented my past. In doing so, however, I had no idea how my future would turn out. Here, I am eternally grateful to my brother Carlton and his wife Jan, for taking me in and guiding me through those very difficult days of uncertainty as I wondered if I had made the right decision. Quite often, I found myself crying out to God for clear directions and instructions as to what my next move should be. But as I began building my relationship with God through prayer, Bible study and attending church, I began to realise that even though things did not make sense to me, God actually had a plan for my life; so I began asking for two things.

The first was that although I had lost a lot of friends during my time of transition since we no longer had anything in common, I wanted to return to the streets and help those who were still living the life I had left behind. I asked God to give me the opportunity and the boldness to speak with the men and women who I knew were looking for peace and love just as I was. God granted me that request by allowing me to accompany my brother as he would go back to the clubs and gambling shops we once frequented. And while in there we were privileged to speak to many people about the love of God.

The second thing I asked God for was a godly wife. I remember praying one day and saying: *"God if you're going to give me a wife, please give me a woman who's a Christian and who truly loves you."* I had experienced the pain of previous relationships which went wrong, so now I just wanted to settle down with a loving wife and together we would serve God.

It was in July 1997, while at a Christian meeting in Holborn, London, that I was introduced to a lady named Norma Ferguson; she had travelled from a town called Milton Keynes, to attend the same meeting. It was a beautiful summer's evening and although the meeting finished late at about 12:30am, it was still quite humid and most people had vacated the main hall to socialise in the foyer. I was standing outside the building, busy handing out flyers to passers-by promoting a gospel event; when my brother came out, calling me into the foyer. He led me to where three ladies were and introduced me to Norma - a long-time friend of his wife – who was with her sister Gee and her friend.

I was so focused on promoting the event that I ignored as we were introduced, hastily saying to Norma, *"Oh, you're so beautiful!"* Then walking off, continuing with what I was doing. That was that!

Norma later told me that she thought I had been rude!

It so happened that the event I had been promoting was an evening of gospel singing and Norma was actually going to be one of the guest singers. We met again a few weeks later on the day of the event. I was excited since I knew we were going to have a good evening. Earlier in the day I had decided to go shopping and ended up at Ridley Market in Dalston. I bought some handkerchiefs and then headed home to get ready. As I was ironing my clothes God spoke to my inner being, instructing me to iron two handkerchiefs; one to use and the other to place in the left inside pocket of the jacket I was going to wear. It seemed a strange instruction; nevertheless I obeyed since I learnt never to question God whenever He spoke to me. That evening I arrived early at the church because with myself there were two other men - John and Lawrence – who were on duty; it was our responsibility to direct people upstairs to the main hall.

By the time Norma arrived with her sister Gee and her friend Michelle, many people were already seated. I recognised them and said hello. She went upstairs and I continued with my duties. The event began but after a while both John and Lawrence said that they were going to walk around the building, so I found myself standing alone at the bottom of the stairs listening to the music coming from the hall. It was at this point that a familiar voice said: *"Go upstairs now and watch your wife play the keyboard."* Again, I thought it to be a strange instruction, seeing that I was unmarried but yet God had told me to go upstairs and watch my "wife" play the keyboard. I am not sure if I ran or flew up the twenty-one steps but I suddenly found myself standing at the back of the hall watching this lady as she sang and played the keyboard.

For a few minutes I stood there, admiring how graceful Norma was as she played and sung; then all of a sudden God said: *"Go and give her the handkerchief which is in the left inside pocket of your jacket."* Now, I always thought of myself as being fairly confident but this instruction caused my knees to buckle. How could I just walk up to the front while this lady sang, giving her my white handkerchief? Surely, I would be making a total fool of myself.

As I pondered what to do, I suddenly remembered that Norma had arrived with two other ladies. I quickly scanned the room and noticed that they were sitting on the right side of the room about half way from the front and Norma was actually at the front on the left side of the room from where I was standing. So, not wanting to disobey God I made my way over to where they sat, handkerchief in hand.

I leant forward and said to Gee, *"Excuse me ma'am but would you give this to the lady playing the keyboard please?"*

To my horror she simply looked at me and said, *"I think you had better do it yourself."*

There was no getting away from it. I needed to face this lady as well as the audience, so I plucked up the courage, walked all the way to the front of the hall, up to the keyboard and placed my handkerchief on it. Norma just lifted her head and looked at me without saying a word; I'm sure that to this day, she thought I was absolutely crazy. Anyway that was the beginning. We spent the next few months getting to know each other and each other's families. I was madly in love – still am - and so was excited knowing that God had actually answered my prayer in such an amazing way. As we knew that God had brought us together, we did not prolong things, but got engaged within three months of meeting and six months later were married on 11th April 1998 in Milton Keynes.

We lived in Stratford in London for a while, settling into married life but with me coming from the "street life" it was often very challenging to make the adjustments. I still struggled to say no to certain invitations from certain friends but I thank God for giving me a godly wife who was patient with me and never gave up on me. She would pray and encourage me until I became stronger and able to decline my friend's invitations.

I have learnt so many valuable lessons from those early days in our marriage.

It is crucial to have God at the centre of everything you do. It is also important that you marry the right person, particularly if you are a Christian because had my wife not been strong in her Christian faith, perhaps this story would have had a different ending. A woman can make or break a man; for me my wife has certainly helped to make me a better person and a stronger Christian. I can say that there have been many times where her timely words of wisdom have lifted me when I felt I was unable to make it and so I am forever grateful to God for bringing Norma Ferguson into my life.

After eleven months living in London, we decided to relocate to Milton Keynes as we felt it would be a good move for us to make and that this was what God wanted. We settled quickly into our new life and began attending Word of Faith Church, in Newton Longville in Milton Keynes under the leadership of Pastor Glen and Lu Ferguson. There, we were able to grow as a couple and discover exactly what God had for our lives. Here I will take a moment to thank Pastor - now Bishop - Glen Ferguson for

Earl and Norma Morgan

being instrumental in my Christian development by his God inspired preaching and teaching.

Our Wedding Day

# Chapter 8 – The Challenge

After relocating to Milton Keynes in March 1999, we rented a two-bedroomed house for a few months but it had always been our desire to buy our own property. As God had always moved miraculously in our lives, we decided that we would trust Him to provide us with our own home by December of that same year. And sure enough on 19th December we had the keys to our first home, moving in a few days later. We were so excited as we decorated and put our own personal touch on it; there were many late nights but we enjoyed ourselves and it was worth the effort.

It was now January 2000 and we needed to put certain important things in place for insurance purposes which meant I needed to have a full medical done. When the results returned from a routine test my doctor contacted me, voicing his concern about traces of blood in my urine. He immediately referred me to a Urology Consultant. An appointment was made for a scan and about a week later, as my wife and I sat in the Consultant's office with his colleagues, we were given the devastating news. The scan had shown that there was a large tumour in my lower abdomen. It was also confirmed to be cancerous and very aggressive and as such I was given two years to live. There were no words to adequately describe how I felt at that very moment.

That prognosis was like a death sentence being pronounced over me and my whole body shook with fear as my wife and I held hands, trying to absorb what we had just been told. As the reality sunk in, my mind went into overdrive. *Would the treatment be successful? What would happen to my dear wife of only two years? How would she cope if I didn't make it?* These torturous thoughts raced through my mind but I suddenly felt - what I can only describe - as an overwhelming sense of peace. I knew it came from God and as it did, I suddenly jumped to my feet, pointed my finger at the Consultant and said, *"Do you believe in Jesus Christ?"*

He answered, *"I believe in God."*

I replied, *"No! No! No! Because where you come from there are many so-called gods but I'm talking about Jesus Christ."*

I wasn't being insulting but I felt such faith and boldness arise in my heart and I went on to say, *"Jesus Christ is going to heal me and you'll be surprised."*

I would never forget the look on the Consultant's face as my question and statements took him by surprise. I imagined his thoughts: *This is a crazy man standing in my office! Here I am, telling him about the possibility of him dying in two years yet still he's saying that Jesus Christ will heal him and surprise us all.*

Anyway, I thanked the Consultant for the information, turned to my wife and said, *"Let's go."*

Heading towards the steps that led downstairs the reality of what I had just been told, suddenly hit me. It was like a solid load of bricks, suddenly weighing me down. The faith and boldness by which I had spoken to the Consultant and his team, only a few moments prior, seemed to disappear as fear gripped my heart. Silent tears began to flow as my wife and I descended the Milton Keynes General Hospital stairs, my legs suddenly buckling as the thought of dying hit home. Desperately, I clung onto my wife as I tried regaining my composure. She, intuitively recognised what was happening and grabbed me, supporting me when I was at my most vulnerable and weakest. When God had blessed me with her, I had not realised how important that was, until that moment. At this point of almost total despair and hopelessness, an inner voice I had become accustomed to, spoke to me.

It said: *"Go and see your Pastor now!"*

I turned to my wife and repeated the words that God had just said. So, we drove in total silence until we reached my Pastor's office in Newton Longville. Once there, I told him what the Consultant had said and immediately my Pastor, Glen Ferguson said: *"Let's pray."* We were in total agreement that day that Jesus would heal me.

Although at times God healed miraculously without any form of human assistance, there were other occasions when He used doctors and medicines to bring about the desired result. In my case, even though, I believed that I was healed after prayer, I still had to use wisdom by going through a month of medical treatment.

Everything was fine and I returned to normality - until 2005.

I once again faced serious health issues to the point that it became very difficult for me to carry out my daily duties at work and home. After many hospital visits and scans, it was discovered that the cancer had returned and spread to my right kidney. This meant having an operation to remove that kidney. This was done at Milton Keynes General Hospital.

Strangely enough though, although things appeared to be getting worse with every hospital visit, I had a quiet assurance that everything would be alright. God had brought me through so much already that I simply believed I would be ok and I found myself on many occasions telling the doctors and other patients that I would be alright and that God would ultimately heal me. Having said that, I couldn't say that it was my great faith that brought me through since there were times when I was weary of the physical and emotional pain, but rather it was God's mercy and His great love for me that kept me alive.

I must mention that even though I was going through such intense suffering, I recall many occasions while in hospital when other patients asked me to pray for them before they went in for surgery or had any form of treatment. Doctors and nurses soon recognised that I was a Christian and that my life was indeed a miracle and they would refer to me as the "miracle man". They also frequently asked me to speak to other patients who had lost hope and this made me realise that in spite of my own personal problems, there was always someone worse off than me, who needed a word of encouragement and comfort; and so I thank God for giving me the strength to do what I had to do in order to help others in their time of need. God also gave me the opportunity to speak to people about His love and they in turn believed and received Jesus Christ into their hearts.

In 2008, because of my failing health I spent at least one week each month for the whole year in hospital, receiving treatment as my left kidney began to fail. Things became so complicated that the doctors resorted to just giving me blood transfusions to keep me alive but stopped all other treatments since they didn't believe that I would survive. At one point, in the space of three weeks, I received thirty-five units of blood and my HB dropped to 0.4 as I kept losing blood. Eventually, it got to the point where I had no option but to have that remaining kidney removed as it too had become infected.

So, in 2010 I went through yet another operation but this time it meant I would then need to begin having dialysis in order to stay alive. After the operation, I actually ended up spending three days and three nights in the Intensive Care Unit in Northampton General Hospital and as far as it went, things were not looking good for me.

I must admit that at that point in my life, I felt confused and my faith was waning somewhat as I knew that there was absolutely nothing that I could do to change what I was experiencing; I was too sick to even pray so all I could do was commit my life into God's hands.

I often tell people when relaying that part of my story that I went into the Intensive Care Unit via the front door but God shut the back one. Therefore, my only way out was to go back through the front door – alive - meaning that if God had not intervened at that time, I wouldn't have made it.

I started having dialysis in March 2010, soon after having my left kidney removed. I was there for one week before being transferred to The Churchill Hospital in Oxford, where my dialysis sessions continued for a further two weeks before being transferred back to Milton Keynes General Hospital. I was told by my Consultant that I would have to have regular dialysis sessions for at least five years before I could even be considered for a kidney transplant due to my medical history.

It is hard to even begin to describe life on dialysis and only those who have experienced it can truly identify. Dialysis is the process of removing excess water and toxins from the blood in people whose kidneys can no longer perform these functions naturally. A dialysis machine actually becomes the patient's kidney or kidneys and as such the patient's blood is removed via the machine's cycle, purified and then returned to the body. My sessions of dialysis were four and a half hours per day, three times a week: Tuesday, Thursday and Saturday initially, but was changed to Monday, Wednesday and Friday. Although this process was keeping me alive, some sessions were so traumatic and frightening because my blood pressure fell dangerously low to the point where I would lose consciousness and need to be resuscitated. On other occasions, my blood pressure would go in the opposite direction, becoming dangerously high. In the end, the constant cramp, nausea and blinding headache become the norm for me.

Since these sessions were mainly during the mornings and I would be so exhausted afterwards, it meant that I could no longer work full-time, so I started working part-time instead. As a man who truly loves his wife, this was very hard to come to terms with and added to my mental and emotional state, but God sustained me and took me through those trying times.

As I recount these experiences, I chose to elaborate on these points because they show not only the depth of suffering I went through but also the magnitude of the miracle that God has done in my life - against all odds.

## Chapter 9 – The Miracle

When I began having dialysis in 2010, I asked my Consultant how long it would be before I could have a kidney transplant; he told me that considering my medical history, I would need to be cancer-free for at least five years before I would even be considered to be put on the transplant list. Although this was not what I wanted to hear, I had to accept the decision of the doctors and go through with regular dialysis.

During those times on the dialysis machine, I would often tell other patients that as soon as I went on the transplant list, my God would do it for me, meaning that I would get a new kidney. This was sometimes met with great scepticism by some who didn't believe in the God that I often spoke about; some even said: *"O yeah? I've heard it all before; I've been waiting for years for my kidney."*

Their remarks, however, did not faze me since I completely trusted the God who had already brought me through the worst because according to the medical reports, I should not have even been alive then.

After four years of dialysis and me telling the doctors that cancer would not return to my body as God had already healed me once and for all; they, the doctors, were not as convinced as I and they told me that I needed to continue being on dialysis but other tests needed to be done. So for the next two years, I was put through some very stringent tests - PET scans, MRI scans and such like - to make sure that everything was indeed fine in my body. Another year went by and I was still having tests done but the results were always the same; everything was fine. At that point in my life I must admit I began to feel somewhat anxious and disappointed with the doctor's decision because they had initially said five years but those five years had turned into seven.

*It must be said that even though the waiting period may be long and things may seem to be going in the opposite direction to what you may believe, do not give up or lose hope. Maintain your confession that things will change and only get better for you. It is also good to always surround yourself with people who encourage and strengthen you, when you do feel like giving up.*

For me, not only did I have a good support network of family and friends, my wife, Norma, was also always there for me, even when I was at my lowest point. I recall many occasions when I was too weak physically, emotionally and spiritually to even help myself but she encouraged me, even dressing me when I could not do it for myself. She fed me when I was unable to do so for myself; spending hours by my bedside while I was in hospital, praying for me when I could not pray for myself, even pushing me in a wheelchair when I could not walk, taking me to church and then back to the hospital and yet still, continuing with her duties at home, work and church.

I want to thank you Babes for being the woman of God that you are; for loving and caring for me. I will always love you and be grateful for your love. Thank you Jesus!

At the beginning of the seventh year the doctors finally gave me the all-clear which meant I could at last be considered to be on the transplant list. But because of the many previous operations, I would first need another operation to ensure that everything was in the right place in preparation for a transplant. So on 21st September 2017, at The Churchill Hospital, Oxford; I had the surgery.

The surgery went well, though it was a long, four and a half hours and later that day I was brought back to the ward where my wife was waiting for me. She stayed with me for a few hours, prayed for me, left and headed back home to Milton Keynes since she was not feeling too well herself. Three days later I began experiencing a lot of pain. I cannot even begin to describe how severe it was but as I lay in the bed in a side room, I began to wonder if I could endure anymore. I was at the point of giving up, wanting to just die since that option seemed to be the easiest one for me. I thought of my dear wife, who was not with me at that moment, and asked God to take care of her if I didn't make it.

I remember feeling very sleepy and seemed to drift away. I was losing consciousness and do not remember much more of that experience except what Gee - my sister-in-law - Norma's sister told me a few days later.

*(Account as relayed by Gee Akinyemi)*

On Sunday, 24th September 2017, immediately after our church service in Milton Keynes, Lawrence, my husband said to me, *"We need to visit Earl and Norma."* Earl and Norma were both sick and in separate hospitals – Norma was in Milton Keynes and Earl, in Oxford. We visited Norma first and after a while Lawrence said, *"We have to leave to go and see Earl in Oxford."* Norma and I suggested to Lawrence that the visit to Earl should be postponed and we could go another day but Lawrence insisted that we had to go that day as he had a very strong impression in his heart. He keyed in the directions to the hospital on his Sat Nav and I did the same on my mobile. We set off but about forty minutes later both Lawrence's Sat Nav and my mobile completely shut down, so we pulled into a petrol station to try to sort out the problem. Lawrence is superb with technology but he could not figure out what was going on as both devices were blank and had no power. After about twenty minutes we decided to continue to the hospital without directions, trusting God would guide us to where we needed to go. Five minutes after we set off, both devices began to work again - how strange! Lawrence and I looked at each other and concluded that this was not a natural occurrence but that we were actually being opposed by some evil force not wanting us to get to the hospital to see Earl.

On arriving at the hospital, we were directed to the ward where Earl was. As we approached the entrance to the room Lawrence and I saw Earl stretched out on the bed, his eyes closed. Lawrence went to the other side of the room and I stood near the door, both of us looking down at our brother.

Earl then began saying, *"Though I walk through the valley of the shadow of death."*

Immediately, God said to me, **"What are you going to do about this?"**

I sensed that Earl was dying and I became very aggressive in my spirit and said to Lawrence, *"Read something from the Bible."* He instantly read Psalms 130 and I began praying. I was being led by the Spirit of God to cancel death and command Earl to live; placing my hand on him until he was still. After a while Earl lifted his right arm, clenched his fist, moved his arm backwards and forwards several times, saying, *"I'm coming back, I'm coming back."*

He then lay motionless, breathing softly.

Lawrence and I stood silent watching him as tears flowed down my cheeks. A few minutes later God said to me, *"You can leave him now."* I stood and waited, then the voice came back to me and repeated, *"You can leave him now."* Lawrence and I held each other's hands, turned and walked away.

Earl is alive and well today – TO GOD BE ALL THE GLORY AND PRAISE!

As this was what some would call an out of body experience, I was not aware that my sister-in-law and her husband had visited me but I do remember feeling as though I was floating as my spirit re-entered my body. At that point I could hear myself shouting *"I'm coming back, I'm coming back"* and as I opened my eyes, I could see that there was a bright light in the room which eventually manifested itself on the wall into the form of Jesus Christ. I knew without a shadow of doubt that it was Jesus my Lord because of the compassion in His eyes as He looked at me and the overwhelming love and peace that I instantly felt. He didn't say anything to me but after a short while the image faded and disappeared.

The doctors and nurses later told me that they also saw a bright light radiating from my room so much so, that they were afraid to enter to find out if I was ok.

I know this may sound strange to some, but believe me, such manifestations are very real.

After that tremendous experience with the Lord, I became aware that all the pain I had previously felt had completely gone. Jesus himself visited me and healed me and I was now ready to go home.

I was discharged from Oxford Hospital a few days later but as my wife was still in Milton Keynes Hospital, I stayed at Lawrence and Gee's home for two weeks after which my wife joined me there; she was discharged from hospital and we stayed a further two weeks. It was while recuperating there that I received a phone call from my nurse in Oxford telling me that I was being put on the transplant list.

I can remember saying to her that I felt like running when she gave me the good news and she said she felt like running with me. It was such exciting news to receive after seven long years of waiting but the amazing part was that the call came only two and a half weeks after I was discharged from Oxford Hospital.

As my wife and I discussed what was happening, we concluded that God was at work and that He was certainly accelerating things for us. Although I was over the moon with excitement, I tried my best to remain calm as I pondered on what the future would be like without having to be dialysed. My wife and I continued to pray and thank God for what He had already done for us but we knew that there was yet a greater miracle to come.

Some people told me that even though I was put on the transplant list, I should not get too excited or build my hopes up too much as the waiting period for a kidney transplant could be many years. I knew from my days of having dialysis that there were patients on the Renal ward who had indeed been waiting a very long time but I somehow had the quiet assurance in my heart that that would not be the case for me. I remember telling them that I believed that God would fast-track things for me; but even though I had been saying that for many years, yet still, I had no idea just how quickly God would actually fulfil His promise to me once I was put on the transplant list.

My wife and I returned to our own home on Saturday 28th October 2017 and for the next few days we rested as we were both going through a healing process. Neither one of us was 100% physically but we did the best we could to help each other as we regained our strength.

I must take a moment to sincerely thank Lawrence and Gee for opening up their beautiful home to my wife and I; for loving and caring for us when we needed it most. I love you dearly.

On Saturday 4th November 2017 I was lying on my bed as my wife was ironing our clothes for church the following day when suddenly the phone rang. Norma answered it and I could tell by her tone that it was a very serious conversation going on but I wondered who it was as it was around 11:00pm. After a few minutes Norma handed the phone to me and whispered that it was the transplant nurse calling from Oxford. I spoke with the nurse and she informed me that I needed to get down to Oxford as soon as possible as a kidney had become available and it could potentially be mine. At that point my heart began to pound with excitement. Could it possibly be my time? Could it possibly be my moment?

As we drove along the winding country roads from Milton Keynes to Oxford, I couldn't help but notice that although there were no other cars on the road for most of the journey and it was very dark, the moon was so bright. It was as though it was guiding us as we journeyed and I believe that it was a sign from God that He was with us.

I really can't even remember saying anything to my wife as my emotions were all over the place; fear, excitement all mixed together but I just wanted to get to the hospital as quickly as possible. By the time we arrived it was 12:40am and we went straight to the ward as we were instructed. I learned that two other couples had also received a phone call just as we had and all three couples would go through the same process that night.

Many blood tests were done throughout the night but by 8:30am the following morning it was confirmed that the kidney was a good match for me and that the transplant would go ahead. Hearing this news was like sweet music to my ears. The long wait was finally over and both my wife and I prayed and thanked God for what He was about to do for us.

So on Sunday 5th November 2017 I had my kidney transplant. When I awoke hours later, the first thing I asked my nurse was *"Did it work?"* to this she replied *"Yes"* and I said *"Thank you Jesus!"* I can also remember seeing my wife standing over me and she was smiling so I knew the operation was a success.

I must point out that by the following day after such a major operation, I was up walking, albeit slowly, but I was walking nonetheless much to the amazement of the doctors and nurses and I was discharged six days later.

The fact that I was only on the transplant list for two and a half weeks was indeed a miracle for which I am truly grateful. Even the staff at the transplant unit were amazed, but all I can say is that with God all things are possible.

Although there were some challenges in the first few months after the transplant, with God's help I have grown stronger and stronger every day and my future is bright. I am so grateful to God for life and I thank Him that against all odds, I'm still here!

Me, After My Transplant

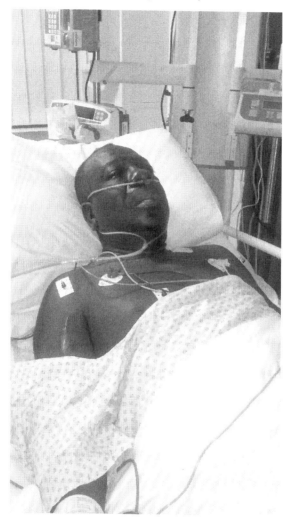

Because God has been so good to me, my desire is to tell my story wherever I go so that He will receive all the praise for what has happened in my life and others will come to know that even if the odds are against you God can do a miracle for you too.

And finally......

As you read through the pages of this book please understand that there is nothing special or unique about me why God should do all the things that He has done in my life. I, just like everyone else, have done wrong and stand in need of His forgiveness. God is not partial, He loves us all but He does require that we open our heart and mind to receive Jesus Christ as our only Lord and Saviour. If you would like to do this, please pray this simple prayer:

**"Dear Lord Jesus, I acknowledge that you are the Son of the living God. Thank you for dying for me and for taking my place on the cross of Calvary. Please forgive me of all my sins and come into my heart through your Holy Spirit. I receive you now as my Lord and Saviour. Thank you Jesus!"**

Now that you have said this prayer, welcome to the family of God. I would encourage you to find a Spirit filled, Bible believing church where you can fellowship with other believers.

Much Love

*Earl*

Me, Sharing My Story

# Chapter 10 – A Wife's Perspective

On 11th April 1998 at 12:15pm, I walked down the aisle in the Oldbrook Christian Centre, Milton Keynes, to take my vows and commit my life to Earl Livingstone Morgan. It was a rainy day and slightly windy but who cared, it was my wedding day and I was happy. As we exchanged our vows to the cheers of family and friends we had no idea of the journey which lay ahead. Many years have passed, twenty in fact during which time we have both had our share of ill health; but my husband in particular has experienced some very challenging health issues. There have been many occasions when I have seen Earl at death's doors yet still God has been faithful to His Word and has kept him alive letting us know that He was with us.

On one particular occasion, when I was with my husband at Northampton General Hospital and he was being wheeled away down the long corridor towards the theatre for yet another operation, kissing him goodbye, I said, *"See you later."* As the door closed behind him, I could go no further and my heart felt as though it would break as I cried out to God in prayer, asking Him to protect my husband. It was at that point and when I turned around, that two ladies stood there. One asked me what was wrong and I told her that my husband had just gone into theatre. She proceeded to ask how long the operation would be and I told her that the doctors said it would take four and a half hours; she then said, *"He will be alright"*, to this I replied, *"I know. I'm a believer."* She informed me that there was a chapel just down the corridor if I needed a quiet place. I turned away for a couple of seconds so that I could wipe my face which was stained with my tears but when I turned around again, the ladies were nowhere in sight. They had disappeared. Now I know that they could not have walked away so quickly so I had to conclude that these were angels sent by God to reassure me that everything would be alright and once they had delivered their message, they just vanished.

The events leading up to my husband's transplant were so miraculous that I need to mention them because of how quickly they happened. After returning home from spending a month at Lawrence and Gee's home recuperating from my own period of illness, God spoke to me and said: ***"Pack Earl's bags and be ready as it won't be long."*** I knew He was referring to the wait on the transplant list. So in obedience to God, I made a checklist of the things I knew Earl would need, putting some things into a travel bag while leaving others on the bed in our spare room with the intention that if we got a call from the Transplant Unit in Oxford, everything would be ready and all I would need to do was throw them into the bag and we would be off.

I mentioned this to my sister Del but she said, *"Norms, pack the bag from now because I know it won't be long; Earl won't have to wait long for his transplant."*

She was right. Exactly one week later on 4th November 2017, we received the call we had been waiting for and the transplant was done the following morning. Earl had only been on the transplant list for two and a half weeks. This we were made to understand was unheard of.

Earl and I have cried together but we have also rejoiced together as we have experienced the miraculous hand of God in our lives on so many occasions. There have been just too many incidences for me to mention in these few pages but all I can say is, *"Father God, I'm truly grateful; thank you for being with us."*

To the wife whose husband is facing health issues, I want to encourage you. Although your husband may be the one experiencing the physical pain, you my sister, are the one who often carries the mental weight of the situation; but the truth of the matter is that with God's help we are often stronger than what we actually think we are and we can bear much more than we think we can. Over the years many people have said to me, *"Norma, you're so strong"* and I often smile because I know it's not a matter of me being strong, because there were times when I have been very weak indeed...But God! How I have made it to this point only God knows as it has not been easy but I am grateful for the support of my family and friends who have stood with us throughout our journey.

So stand with your man and watch God do a miracle for you.

May this book touch and transform many lives.

Norma

# Chapter 11 – Testimonials

## Carol Campbell – Nurse and friend

I have known Earl for many years but really got to know him when he started his dialysis treatment in Milton Keynes Dialysis Unit where I was a Dialysis Nurse. Like any other human being, he had his moments but I believe he dug deep at times and commanded his will to be stronger especially for "Babes" (his wife) who we nurses identified as being his rock. Overall he was a very jovial and positive thinking person; he was and still is the sort of person who would make lemonade from the lemons life threw at him and was always sporting that infectious smile that drew everyone to him.

Earl and the team of nurses, definitely shared moments of joy and laughter; some really good jokes, but we also cried when a member of the dialysis family passed away. RIP to our brothers and sisters.

Having dialysis is a very serious thing and there were many anxious moments along the road. The temperamental machines, the dialysis access, Earl hated the one in the neck so he would always pray, *"Dear Lord, guide the hand of the nurse who is going to put my needles in me."*

He bought his own spice to the mix, which was a good thing. Earl was just Earl; always encouraging everyone, the new patients in particular and - oh yes - even the nurses got our portion. I remember one particular Christmas when he walked in out of the freezing cold and without warning just burst into a beautiful carol. We were all gobsmacked as we did not even know that he could sing but it certainly cheered everyone up and his gesture was the headline news of the unit for weeks following; such was his disposition.

My desires for Earl is that he will be continually blessed and have a full life with his "Babes". Dream big my brother as you continue your walk with God xx.

**Sam Monrose – Dialysis patient and friend**

While being on the same dialysis sessions as Earl, I have seen him go through some hard times. One incident I can recall was when he had a very bad reaction to a particular medication. All the alarms on his dialysis machine went off and doctors and nurses came running to his bedside drawing the curtain around him as the colour drained from his face and he passed out but thank God they managed to revive him.

I spoke to him later that morning as I was in the bed opposite him and asked if he was ok. He replied that he was feeling bad but he knew that God was watching over him. Such was his demeanour, one of faith in his God. In spite of everything, he never lost hope and always had a positive attitude even when things were not going well.

Although going through pain himself, his words were always so uplifting to me and the other patients, encouraging us all to hold on to our faith and that God is good.

One thing I will always remember is that Earl maintained that he would get a new kidney one day and that Jesus would do it for him, but in the beginning of 2017 Earl told us all that he would get his new kidney before Christmas and sure enough he did in November just as he had said. I am so happy for him.

**Donna Akuffo - Dialysis Patient and Friend**

Earl and Norma have always struck me as people of faith and determination.

I met Earl by accident really as he was initially on the alternate dialysis treatment schedule, Tuesdays, Thursdays and Saturdays and then he changed to the same shift that I was on - Mondays, Wednesdays and Fridays.

He was quiet but I always felt that he had a lot of meaningful things to say. One of the most important things Earl ever said to me was: *"Always pray, for better times were on the way."* He also constantly invited me to visit his church. It took me five years to take up that offer!

Earl brought a ray of sunshine to The Milton Keynes Renal Unit and during his time there he really lit up our surroundings with his beautiful smile to such an extent that we often forgot that we were actually having treatment with needles and all that dialysis entails; sickness, cramps, low blood pressure etc; we were all just good friends, laughing, chatting and spending time together.

His attitude was always so positive because he knew in his heart that the Lord was going to make his miracle happen. His deep faith spoke volumes. For Earl, it was a certainty, a promise from God that would not be broken and so with his loving wife Norma by his side, they persevered to see the Lord's glorious work and sure enough, a kidney transplant happened for him.

Earl gave me hope, cheered me up and made me laugh so much.

I know for a fact that Earl and Norma have always kept me in their prayers. They have helped me through the best and worst times. They gave me confidence to face each new challenge and also to rely on the Lord to help me to find peace where I did not have it before. They have had such a positive effect on my life; for this I am deeply grateful. Earl's life is a testament to the power of God; when doctors had written his very existence off, putting a limit on his life and happiness, but Earl said, *"No way!"*

He is indeed loved and respected by all.

## Levi Francis

I first met Earl Morgan in September 2014 shortly after my wife and I joined Faith Dimensions Church, in Milton Keynes; where he and his wife Norma were already attending. What struck me most about him was his attitude of always being grateful to God regardless of his health issues; he just seemed to be able to praise God even when he was not feeling 100%.

As someone who has faced health challenges in the past, seeing this has certainly encouraged and inspired my faith in God and Uncle Earl *(as I often call him)* has shown through his life, that we can with God's help, go through difficult times successfully.

I believe this kind of attitude is something that God honours and requires of us all.

His passion to share his faith with others is admirable and so is his love and support for his wife which is very rare these days.

My desire is that God will sustain and enable him to fulfil his purpose on earth and that he will stop running away from the challenge to play me at dominos so that we can finally determine who the real champion is!

**Oke – A Friend**

I have known Earl Morgan for over fourteen years during which time we have attended the same church in Milton

Keynes. I call him Deacon Earl because he has proven himself to be a man after God's own heart; strong in his faith and does not take no for an answer concerning God's business. He has remained consistent and he is a lovely man.

He has influenced me in so many ways but just to mention a few I would have to say he has shown me through his life, how to continue serving God faithfully in spite of life's challenges, how to take care of others and how to love and take care of my wife.

My prayer for Deacon Earl is that God will keep him strong and that he will finish well. May God's blessing continually be upon him and may he live in divine health.

# Earl and Norma Morgan

Me, With My Brother Carlton

Me, Earl Morgan

Printed in Great Britain
by Amazon

56537462R00056